PLANET DEXTER

A Satellite of Addison-Wesley
Publishing Company

Balls

The Book with Bounce!

by The Editors of Planet Dexter and Bill Haduch with David Williams
Illustrated by Jack Keely

Addison-Wesley Publishing Company

Reading, Massachusetts   Menlo Park, California   New York
Don Mills, Ontario   Harlow, England   Amsterdam   Bonn
Sydney   Singapore   Tokyo   Madrid   San Juan
Paris   Seoul   Milan   Mexico City   Taipei

Through the Addison-Wesley TRI∆NGLE Program, Planet Dexter books are available from your bookseller at special discounts for bulk purchases; or, contact the Corporate, Government, and Special Sales Department at Addison-Wesley Publishing Company, One Jacob Way, Reading, MA 01867, or call 1-800-238-9682.

Book concept based on a CD-ROM proposal by David Hautzig.

Illustrations by Jack Keely
Cover design by Suzanne Heiser
Interior design by C. Shane Sykes
Set in various sizes of Agenda and Helvetica

And Now a Message from Our Corporate Attorney:

"Neither the publisher nor the author shall be liable for any damage that may be caused or sustained as a result of conducting any of the activities in this book, *Balls: The Book with Bounce*, without specifically following instructions, conducting the activities without proper supervision, or ignoring the cautions contained in the book."

ISBN 0-201-48986-4

1 2 3 4 5 6 7 8 9-GC-0099989796
First printing, February 1996

"One of the advantages of bowling over golf is that you very seldom lose a bowling ball."

—Don Carter, professional bowler

Dedication

to Liz

IT'S A BALL WORLD AFTER ALL

You live on a big one. The sky is filled with them. You eat them with spaghetti. Pirates use them to sink each other's ships. They help make your chairs swivel and your vacuum cleaner run. You watch grown men and women hit them and throw them and catch them for millions of dollars. Dogs chase them for free.

The subject we're kicking around, of course, is the ball—that wonderfully familiar object that can be so strange. It bounces, it spins, it rolls in any direction. And it stores and transfers energy to other objects.

Use your eyeballs to scan the dictionary and you'll find that a "ball" is an object that is spherical or almost spherical. Great. What's that mean? Well, a ball is like a circle that's always a circle, no matter how you look at it. Think about a POG for a minute. If you look at it straight on, it's a circle. If you look at it at an angle, it's an oval. If you look at it from the edge, it's a straight line. Weird. Same thing with refrigerators and shoes and soda cans. They all change shape depending on how you look at them. But a ball is always a circle, no matter how you look at it (unless it's one of those screwy footballs!).

Anyway, it's a toy, it's a moon, it's a tool, it's a **ball**.

Let's roll!

Get to Know Your **Balls**

Although the **balls** supplied with *"Balls: The Book with Bounce"* come from Planet Dexter, they have been designed to work within Earth's gravity parameters.

Drop one of the solid Super**balls** on a hard floor. Hear the satisfying "thunk" sound? Note that it bounces back almost to its original height.

Now, drop your hollow Ping-Pong **ball** onto a hard floor. Hear the higher-pitched "click" sound and note that the Ping-Pong **ball's** bounce isn't as high as the Super**ball's**.

When you're goofing around with this book, be sure to try **balls** other than those that come with this book! Try golf **balls**, basket**balls**, even your Dad's bowling **ball**.

Test Your Balls

A Superball dropped from a height of 48 inches onto a concrete floor returns to a height of about 44 inches on the first bounce; however . . .

A Ping-Pong ball dropped from a height of 48 inches onto a concrete floor returns to a height of only about 32 inches. Hmmm. . . .

Why? What's going on here?

Think of it this way. Just before the balls are dropped, they have "potential energy." As the balls fall they gain "kinetic energy" (energy related to motion). When the balls hit the floor, the particles in the balls squeeze together, like tiny springs. The balls bounce when all these particles spring back to their original shapes. A Superball, made of lots of squeezable particles, bounces higher than a Ping-Pong ball composed of a hard shell and air.

Have A Ball!

This is not your usual book-with-balls. You are not restricted by the traditional rules of book use. Start at the beginning. Start at the end. Read it from across the park with a pair of binoculars. Wait for the wind to turn the pages. Sleep with it under your pillow and see if you can recite it in the morning.

You are about to enter a world of invisible forces that will spin you and bounce you and rock you and roll you. Knowing ball stuff will astound others. Adults will think you're really intelligent and let you stay up late to watch shows on PBS (then when they leave the room—click!—flip the channel to *The Beverly Hillbillies*).

Bounce Some Ideas Around

The Editors of Planet Dexter would love to know what's inside that big ball atop your shoulders. So if anything in this book makes you go "HEY, WOW!" or "HEY, NO WAY!," we want to know! Send us your letters, pictures, drawings, and maybe we'll send you some of ours! Or send us one of your old T-shirts and maybe we'll send you one of our new T-shirts!

Write:

- The Editors of Planet Dexter
  Addison-Wesley Publishing Company
  One Jacob Way
  Reading, MA 01867

- Or FAX us at (617) 944-8243

- Or punch us up on the Internet at pdexter@aw.com or America Online at PDexter.

Ball State University, founded in 1918, is a public university offering undergraduate and graduate programs.

If, as David Letterman did, you want to go to college here,
1) study this book thoroughly,
2) save up lots of money, then
3) contact Ruth Vedvik, Director of Admissions, Ball State University, Muncie, IN 47306.

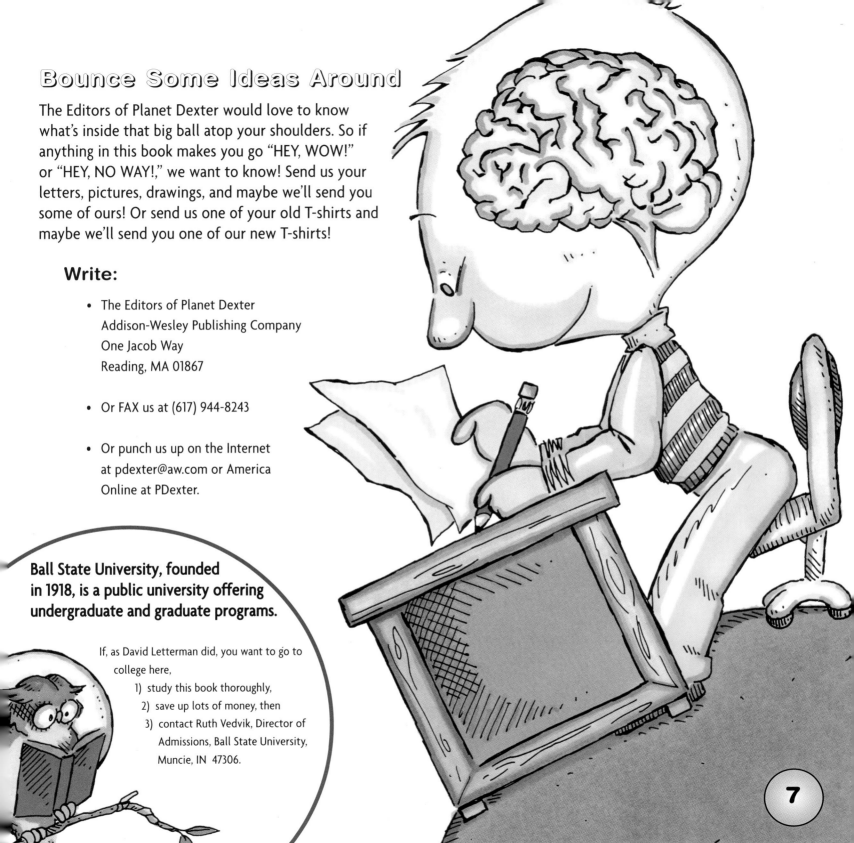

7

A TOUGH QUESTION

Question:

How far can you throw a ball?

Answer:

Might depend on lots of things, like—

- type of ball
- ball's weight
- wind (quickly developing hurricanes in your neighborhood)
- how much sleep you got last night
- whether you throw it overhand, underhand, or sidearm
- greasy fingers (are you in the middle of a large order of French fries?)
- your attitude
- whether you kept the ball in the freezer, next to the ice cream, for the last 37 days
- whether you can find the ball after it hits the ground*
- a large bird thinks the ball is a flying egg and plucks it out of the air before it hits the ground.

In the men's Olympic shot-put, the shot, or metal ball, weighs 16 pounds. That's one HEAVY ball. The world record for throwing a shot put is about 75 feet, 10 inches.

A baseball weighs about 5 ounces. The world record for throwing one is 445 feet, 10 inches.

*In golf you're penalized two strokes if you can't find your ball. . . .
  so why aren't you rewarded two strokes if you find somebody else's lost ball?

See? The heavy ball goes a short distance;
the lighter ball goes a much longer distance.
Sooooo . . . How about a Ping-Pong ball?
It's amazingly light, weighing just a few grams.
You should be able to throw a Ping-Pong ball about a mile, right?
Go ahead, try it. Hmmm. What's going on here?
SEE WHY IT'S A TOUGH QUESTION??????

Why can't you throw a Ping-Pong ball as far as a baseball if you can throw a baseball much farther than a shot put?

This question has to do with momentum, which has to do with mass.

Mass is the amount of matter (stuff!) in an object. The mass of an object is constant; it won't change regardless of where in the world you are—at the top of a mountain or along the Jersey Shore at low tide, up in the attic or down in the basement. Mass is not affected by gravity the way weight is.

(Note: if you don't like this definition, try the one on page 47!)

Now, **momentum**. Momentum is the strength of an object's motion. That strength depends upon the object's mass and speed. For example, the faster you throw a ball, the more momentum it has, so the more impact it has when it hits something. For example, Fred throws a ball at some glass—BLAM!—Fred's ball does some damage. If Helen then throws a ball with twice the mass of Fred's, even at half the speed, it'll—BLAM—cause the same damage that Fred's did.

Thus, **the answer**. The Ping-Pong ball has so little mass that it can't gain enough momentum to overcome the forces of air resistance and gravity. A shot put, on the other hand, has such a large mass that gravity easily drags and slows it down, destroying its momentum. However, a baseball is just the right balance of mass and achievable velocity for it to gather enough momentum to be thrown fairly far.

How far can you—

- **throw a Superball vs. a Ping-Pong ball when there's no wind?**

- **throw a Superball vs. a Ping-Pong ball INTO a heavy wind?**

- **throw a Superball and a Ping-Pong ball at the same time from the same hand?**

- **throw a wadded-up ball of newspaper?**

- **throw a wadded-up ball of newspaper that's been soaked with water?**

- **throw up if you're really sick?**

With the help of a $50,000 catapult now under development, the International Hurling Society ("Dedicated to the art, science, and history of throwing things") of Fort Worth, Texas, is planning to hurl a car 250 yards (that's the length of two and a half football fields!). The group has already tested smaller catapults, including a 25-foot model that can fling a toilet about 150 yards. Dr. John Quincy, a dentist and spokesperson for the International Hurling Society, notes, "The sight of a toilet flying almost 200 yards through the air is one of the most magnificent things I've ever seen."

If you go to the circus you might see a dog or seal rewarded handsomely for jumping up and sitting on a big colorful ball. BIG DEAL! You sit and walk and sleep and eat on a big colorful ball (THE EARTH!!!) all day and all night and nobody ever throws you a fish.

THE PENDULUM OF FEAR

Benjamin Franklin risked his life for science.
He flew a kite in a thunderstorm.
So how's 'bout you risking your nose for science?

Better yet, how about just giving the illusion of risking your nose for science? "What bravery!" your friends will exclaim, applauding and carrying you around on their shoulders (well, maybe). Go ahead, enjoy the acclaim. There's no reason to reveal that you and your nose are perfectly safe from **THE PENDULUM OF FEAR.**

Here's what to do—

1. Use a rubber band, a Superball, and about five feet of string to construct a pendulum.

2. Wrap the rubber band around the ball tightly (it may take several wraps) and then slip the string under the rubber band.

3. Tape the string to the top of a door frame. Make sure the ball rests at about bellybutton level.

4. Grasp the ball and walk backward, until the ball is just touching your nose comfortably.

5. When you're ready, let the ball go, letting it swing of its own weight. Don't push it, and don't move your head. The pendulum will swing out and begin its return journey, heading right for your— now be brave . . . your . . . NOOOOOOOOOOO!

Don't move!

Provided you haven't added any energy to the pendulum by pushing it,

IT'LL SWING SHORT OF YOUR NOSE EVERY TIME!

It can't help it. Every time the pendulum swings it loses some of its energy to air resistance and its swing gets shorter and shorter.

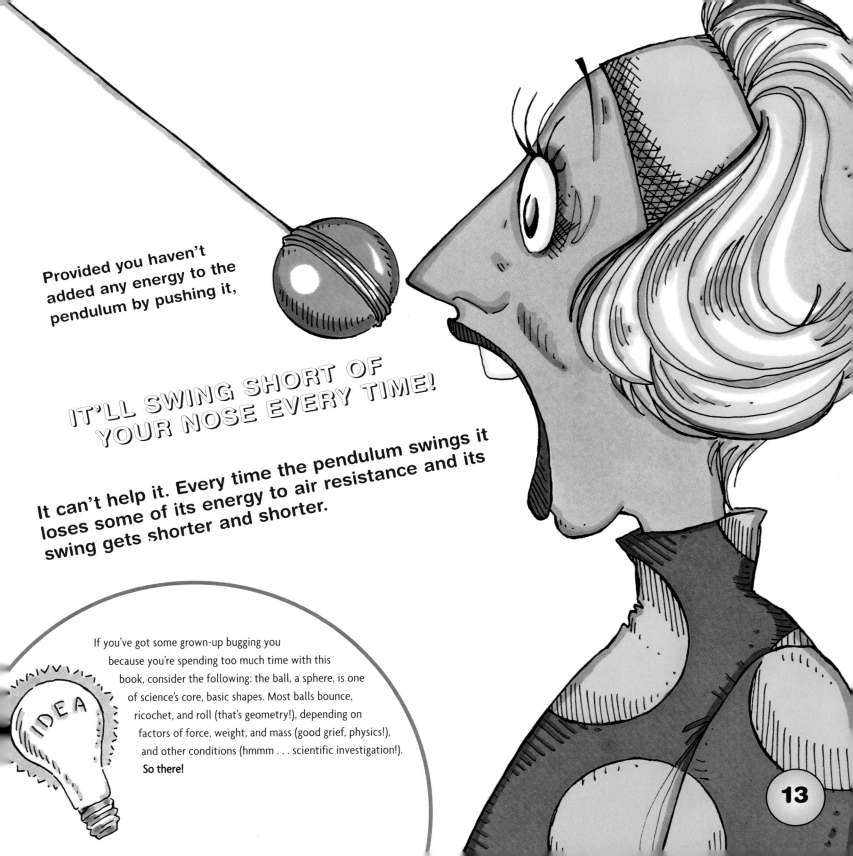

If you've got some grown-up bugging you because you're spending too much time with this book, consider the following: the ball, a sphere, is one of science's core, basic shapes. Most balls bounce, ricochet, and roll (that's geometry!), depending on factors of force, weight, and mass (good grief, physics!), and other conditions (hmmm . . . scientific investigation!). **So there!**

IDEA

13

DO YOU NEED GLASSES?

Yes, you do.
But coffee mugs will work just as well.

HIGHLY HELPFUL SUGGESTION:

**Do not break a glass!!
Before proceeding any further, you
better check with whoever's in charge
of the glasses in your life.**

The idea is to drop a Superball
into an empty drinking glass or mug
on the floor from about shoulder height—
and have the ball stay in the glass.

Lucille Ball is considered
the world's most-watched
television performer—
I Love Lucy is syndicated in
over 70 countries! When the
zany redhead died in 1989, it
was not a good day for balls.

14

It's trickier than it sounds.

**Sure, aiming is hard enough,
but the real challenge is the ball's behavior
after it bounces.**

- If the bottom of the glass is absolutely flat, the ball is likely to bounce straight out.

- If the bottom of the glass is rounded, the ball may bounce out at an angle.

- Would spinning the ball as you drop it help? Or does that just make you miss the glass totally?

- What if the ball hits the inside wall of the glass before it hits the bottom?

Practice. Experiment. Devise a game out of it. Name the game. Then pretend you're a grown-up and write all sorts of complicated rules and regulations for your game. Tell us about your game and maybe we'll you send something in return, or use your game in the upcoming book, *Planet Dexter's Best Games Ever!* See page 7 for how to contact us.

Duck!

The fastest ball game is said to be *Jai Alai* (Hi Lie), in which players fling a small ball from gloves that look like baskets. The ball flies at speeds recorded as high as 188 miles per hour!

THE BOUNCING GRANDMA

Since George Washington was the "Father of Our Country," that makes George Washington's mother the "Grandmother of Our Country," right? And guess what?—George's mother's name was Ball . . . Mary Ball.

"He sometimes throws and catches a ball for hours with his aide-de-camp."
—anonymous soldier, regarding George Washington's behavior at Valley Forge

Ball, Louisiana, is apparently the only town in America named simply "Ball." It is considered to be a well-rounded place.

Wow!

Just imagine if George used his mom's last name instead of his dad's!:

- The capital of the United States would be Ball, D.C.

- The Washington Monument would be the Ball Monument, and it would probably be much rounder.

- Every town would have a Ball Street.

- Every February we would celebrate Ball's Birthday.

- It would be Seattle, Ball.

- The nightly news guys would say "Reporting tonight from Ball . . ."

- Instead of Washingtonians, people who live in D.C. would be called Ballites. Or Ballinians? Or maybe, better yet, **Balloons**?

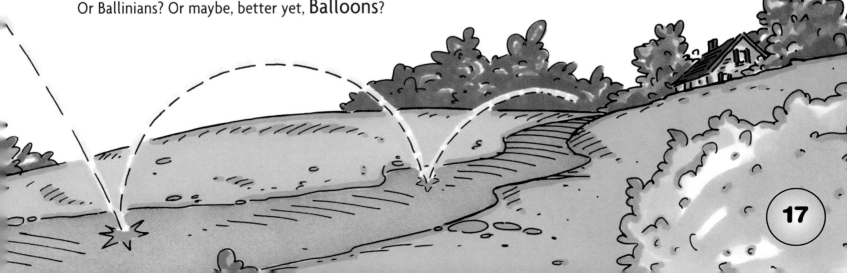

THE LARGE
& SMALL OF IT

What's the LARGEST ball you're ever likely to see?

That'd be Betelgeuse (bee tull juice), one of the largest and brightest stars we know about. This reddish ball of burning gas can be found at the right shoulder of the constellation Orion.* Betelgeuse is HUMONGOUS! It's 360 million miles across! In comparison, our sun is less than one million miles across. If Betelgeuse was in the middle of our solar system, it would completely engulf our sun, plus cover up Mercury, Venus, Earth, and Mars.

The smallest ball you're ever likely to encounter is on the tip of every ballpoint pen. Check it out. This tiny, hard metal ball rolls smoothly along as you write, transferring ink to the paper.

Now, want to do something weird? Some night hold up the tip of a ballpoint pen alongside Betelgeuse as we see it from earth. The tiny ballpoint tip and the mighty Betelgeuse will appear to be about the same size!

*No, no, no! We're not going to tell you where to find Orion in the night sky. Check your bookshelves, an encyclopedia, head for the library, go on-line, stuff like that. Or, OK, annoy your really smart Uncle Fred until he tells you.

Louis XI, King of France from 1461 to 1483, had a billiard ball table.

OVER THE EDGE

A ball game in which no one touches the ball!

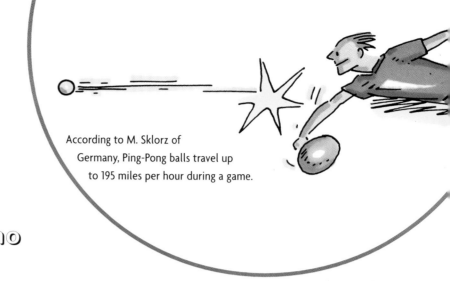

According to M. Sklorz of Germany, Ping-Pong balls travel up to 195 miles per hour during a game.

What? No hands? No feet? No bouncing balls off players' foreheads? Nope, not at all . . . the only thing that touches the ball is a lot of hot air.

Just run a line of tape along a tabletop, dividing the tabletop in half. Each single player or team gets half of the tabletop to defend and everybody gets a drinking straw. Flip a coin to see which side gets to drop the Ping-Pong ball on the center of the tape line from one hand's height. When the ball stops bouncing, the players or teams use their straws to try to blow the ball off opposite side of the table. Each ball "over the edge" scores a point.

Remember, once the ball is in play, no one can touch it in any way— including touching it with the straw. Touching the ball awards the other side a point. The first side to reach 11 points wins.

KARATE BALL

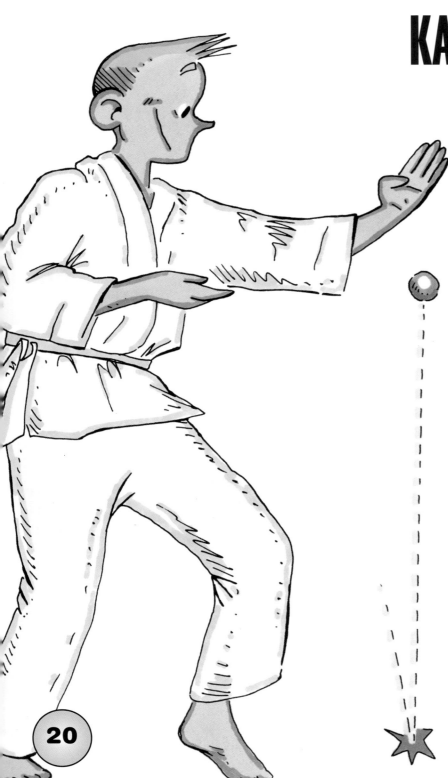

Did you ever watch a karate expert break a board with one chop of a bare hand? Did you ever spend the next few days with a sore hand because you're no expert? **Ouch!**

Well, put away the bandages. Here's a way to amuse yourself and your friends with karate chops—and still be able to use your hands to play guitar like Eddie Van Halen the next day.

Just drop one of your Superballs on an open area of hard floor. While the ball is up at the highest point of its bounce, make it spin by giving it a good karate chop on one side. Chop straight down, using your hand like a meat cleaver. If you want to be dramatic, yell "Kee-Yah!" or "Dex-Ter!" or even "Fung-Goo!"

Now, what does the ball do? Back and forth, back and forth, right? Bouncing, bouncing, back and forth. It's not only karate, *IT'S HYPNOTISM!*

What's going on here?

The energy in the spinning ball doesn't disappear just because the ball hits the floor. In fact, the spin of the ball changes direction every time the ball hits the floor.

Ping-Pong Boomerang

Put a little spin on your PING-PONG BALL to see a real cool boomerang effect. Just put your Ping-Pong ball on a hard floor or tabletop and slap your index finger down along side it. You'll see it scoot off in one direction, but its spin will soon have it coming back at you.

CAN'T IT MAKE UP ITS MIND?

The Chinese Nationalist Golf Association claims that the Chinese were first playing golf—they call it *ch'ui wan* (the ball-hitting game)—way back in the third or second century B.C.

DOWN THE TUBES

There are millions and millions of paper towel rolls used in the U.S. every day. Your job? Collect about five or ten or twenty of the empty tubes. That doesn't sound so hard, does it? Paper towel tubes are great because they're all 11 inches long. And their openings are always 1-3/4 inches wide. That's the perfect width for your Superballs and Ping-Pong balls to roll through!

With scissors and tape and a little imagination, you can make amazing tube and gutter systems that can guide your Dexter Balls down walls, around corners, through rooms, across floors. The only power required is gravity, available on planets everywhere.

You can start out small and expand your system as you get more tubes. Maybe you can transfer balls from one room to another. Go for distance! Go for speed! Go for donuts!

If you come up with something really cool, send us a picture. Maybe we'll send you something in return (like a T-shirt, or an officially autographed paper towel tube). See page 7 for how to contact us.

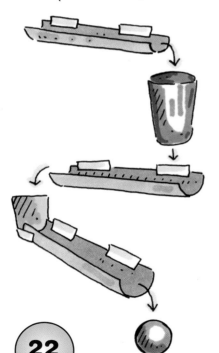

- Remember, the steeper the angle, the faster the roll. Can you arrange your tubes and gutters for maximum roll time?

- If the balls tend to overshoot the next ramp, use strips of stiff paper to make "stopper" panels for trouble spots. Junk mail is full of stiff paper.

- Using a paper cup with the bottom cut out at the end of a ramp can send the ball into a wild and wacky spiral before it drops down onto the next ramp.

- What rolls through your ramps and tubes faster—a Superball or a Ping-Pong ball?

Why?

THE AMAZING TRUTH ABOUT BEACH BOWLING

People play a lot of games on the beach. Frisbees, beach balls, and burying-hairy-old-men-in-the-sand are big favorites. But why no bowling?

Some people claim the problem is bowling shirts—their bright colors tend to fade in the hot sun and salt water. Others blame pelicans and their uncontrollable fondness for bowling pins. Yet others blame it all on the demise of dodo birds, who were great at setting pins.

What do you think? Why no beach bowling? Here's an idea. Roll your Planet Dexter Superballs—as you would roll a bowling ball—on the following surfaces and check the appropriate boxes.

	Suitable for Bowling	Not Suitable for Bowling	Shirt Fades	Pelicans Appear
Hard, smooth floor: linoleum, tile, or wood	❑	❑	❑	❑
Rug or carpet	❑	❑	❑	❑
Grass	❑	❑	❑	❑
Sandy beach or sandbox	❑	❑	❑	❑

What's the best surface? Why?* Is it a matter of Pelicans? Bowling shirts? Pelicans wearing bowling shirts?? Let us know what you've concluded (see page 7 for how to contact us) and maybe we'll send you a T-shirt, a bowling shirt, or our sincere gratitude.

*Do you suppose, by any chance, it might have something to do with the friction of the individual sand granules, which tend to drain the energy from the ball as it rolls?

JUST YOLKING AROUND

It's always good to start the day off with a stunt—and here's a dandy.

Remember we said a ball could be "almost spherical?" Well, this stunt "revolves" around the difference between two almost spherical eggs—one hard boiled, the other uncooked. They look alike, they feel alike, they smell alike. But . . .

Getting Ready

First—and you have to do this ahead of time—you'll need a hard-boiled egg. Be sure to enlist some adult help because stoves and boiling water can be dangerous. Boil the egg for at least 10 minutes. After the egg cools, just put it in the refrigerator. Keep it separate from the uncooked eggs, so you can tell it apart when you're ready for some fun.

The Set-Up

Some morning, ask some grumpy grown-up—the sleepier and more unsuspecting, the better—"Is it true that adults lose finger coordination after age 25?"

"Huh?"

You quickly reply, "I heard that adults can't even spin eggs!"

Some grumps will simply give you that annoyed, burning look they so pride themselves in; better yet, others will protest, "Of course I can spin eggs!"

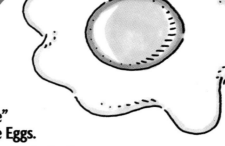

The Hoot

At this point simply retrieve your boiled egg and any uncooked egg from the refrigerator. Using your thumb and fingers, spin your BOILED egg on a plate. It will spin and spin.

"Can you do that?" you ask the grump, handing him or her the UNCOOKED egg.

The grump will grab the uncooked egg from your hand and try. And try and try and try. The uncooked egg may wobble. It may lurch. It may teeter. But it won't spin nearly as well as your boiled one.

The Chase

At some point the now-fully-awake grump will reach over, give your egg a spin, and realize it's a trick. Simply skedaddle out of the kitchen door yelling back over your shoulder,

"When you spin the shell of an uncooked egg, the loose liquid white and yolk inside want to stay still.

That's inertia!

The white and yolk of a boiled egg are solid. They do whatever the shell does!
Even a kid knows that!"

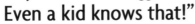

A TOP TEN BALLS LIST

Our List (The Editors of Planet Dexter)

Your List*

#10)	**Football**	**#10)** _____
#9)	**Baseball**	**#9)** _____
#8)	**Campbell's Baked Beans and Balls**	**#8)** _____
#7)	**Squash Ball**	**#7)** _____
#6)	**Fred W. Ball of Dayton, Ohio**	**#6)** _____
#5)	**Nerfball**	**#5)** _____
#4)	**Bocci Balls**	**#4)** _____
#3)	**Ball State University**	**#3)** _____
#2)	**Matzo balls**	**#2)** _____
#1)	**Dexter Balls!!!**	**#1)** _____

*Send us a copy of your "Top Ten Balls List." Maybe we'll send you something back—like ten bocci balls; or a bowling ball autographed by Fred W. Ball of Dayton, Ohio; or a Planet Dexter T-shirt. Or maybe we'll include your list in the yet to be published *Planet Dexter's Book of Top Ten Lists*.
See page 7 for how to contact us.

Until then!

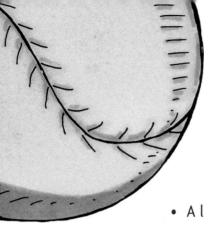

Baseball Weirdness

- At New York's Shea Stadium, on April 12, 1967, Dion James's fly ball hit and killed a dove before falling to the ground for a double.

- A list of every player named "Ball" who ever played professional baseball:
  Art Ball
  Jim Ball
  Neal Ball

- Before every professional baseball game, the umpires are responsible for inspecting 13 dozen brand new balls and roughing them with "rubbing mud."

- On September 14, 1989, 16-year-old Travis Johnson held nine regulation baseballs in one hand.

- One day in 1945, at Boston's Fenway Park, when A's right fielder Hal Peck threw a ball to home plate, it hit a pigeon and fell to the second baseman who tagged out a very surprised Skeeter Newsome.

- In 1957, Glen Gorbous threw a baseball 445 feet, 10 inches. No one's ever thrown it farther.

- Baseball is the only major team sport in which scoring is not done with the ball. Think about it. In football, basketball, or even hockey with its weird puck, the ball actually scores.

The Wiffle ball was invented by a young boy and his brother in their back yard because they couldn't throw a curve ball. Since then over two billion (!) Wiffle balls have sold worldwide.

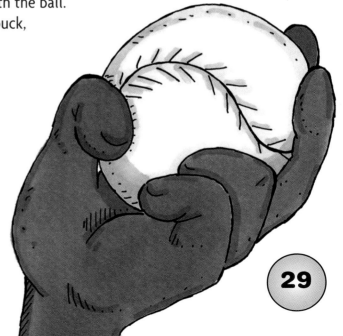

THE SALTY SECRET OF CANNONBALL BOB

There must be something very appealing about being shot out of a cannon into a tank of water. Maybe it's the smell of the gunpowder or the roar of the crowd, or the refreshing splash when you plunge headlong into the tank.

One thing's certain, though—hitting the bottom of the tank would leave a real lump on your head. So how does somebody like Cannonball Bob Stigowatz, Professional Human Cannonball, captivate the crowd while keeping his head lump-free?

Try this. Get two bowls of plain water. Float a Superball in each. Observe how high or low each ball sits in the water (how much of each ball is sticking out of the water). Now add salt to one of the bowls. Keep adding until no more salt will dissolve. Notice anything about the ball sitting in the salted water compared to the one sitting in the non-salted water?

No?

OK, keep reading.

30

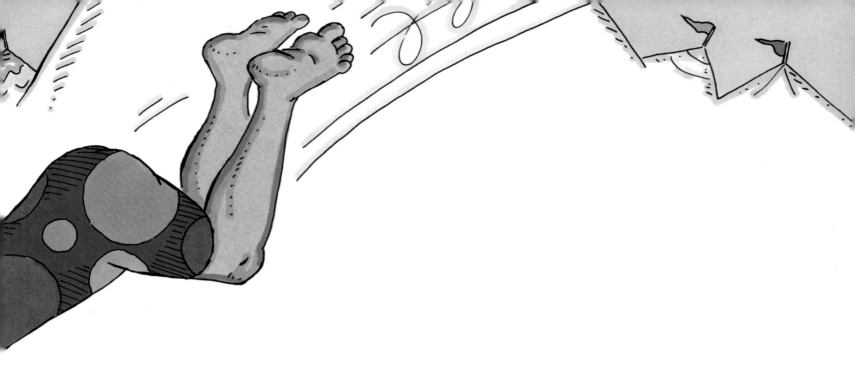

The Great Salt Lake in Utah is one of the saltiest bodies of water on earth.
Swimmers report an ability to simply float on their backs, as if on an inflatable raft.

Why?

It's the salt. It increases the density of the water.
Because your body's density remains the same, you float higher in the denser water.

And that's the key to Bob's undamaged head.

HE NEVER HITS HIS HEAD ON THE BOTTOM OF THE TANK BECAUSE HE ALWAYS SALTS HIS WATER JUST BEFORE COUNTDOWN!

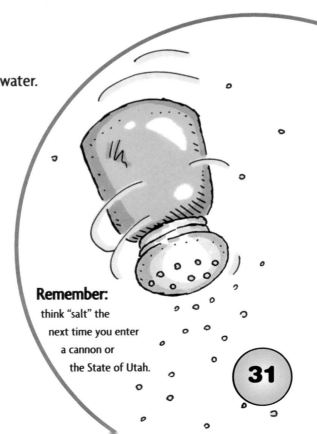

Remember: think "salt" the next time you enter a cannon or the State of Utah.

31

TAKE ME OUT TO THE BALL NAME

Take a break, grab some peanuts and Cracker Jacks and see if you can crack this crazy Balltrivia Baseball Quiz.

On the left side you'll see the names of some current baseball teams. On the right are the former names of those teams. See if you can match up the current and former names. Yup, there are more than enough former names. Some teams were renamed more than once (answers on page 33).

CURRENT
Names

Astros

Cubs

Giants

Indians

Pirates

Tigers

Yankees

FORMER
Names

A.   Alleghenies

B.   Colts

C.   Colt .45s

D.   Creams

E.   Forest Citys

F.   Gothams

G.   Highlanders

H.   Dextermites

I.   Hilltoppers

J.   Naps

K.   Orphans

L.   Spiders

Drive 'Em Nuts . . . Throw 'Em A Curve

Pitchers love them, batters dread them. It's the curve ball and here's how it works.

The pitcher throws the ball so that it spins just about a quarter of the way around on its way to the plate. That's all—just about one quarter of a complete turn. During this turn the THREADS on the ball create just enough wind turbulence to make the ball flutter and curve. It moves about a foot off course, driving the batter crazy.

For years, pitchers threw curves and asked no questions—nobody really knew what was happening with the ball. Then scientists stepped in with wind tunnels, big government grants, and slow motion photography.

BLAM!—another mystery knocked out of the park by science.

Answers:

Houston Astros: (C) Colt .45s

Chicago Cubs: (B) Colts, (K) Orphans

San Francisco Giants: Played in New York as the (F) Gothams

Cleveland Indians: (E) Forest Citys, (J) Naps, (L) Spiders

Pittsburgh Pirates: (A) Alleghenies

Detroit Tigers: (D) Creams

New York Yankees: (G) Highlanders, (I) Hilltoppers

(you didn't really fall for "Dextermites" . . . did you?)

SHALL WE DANCE?

Dancing appears to be one of the truly unexplainable forces of nature. Some people can't help but dance. Others simply can't at all. One person rocking back and forth at a party can soon send a roomful of people into a frenzy. Why? Scientists believe there may be some connection to the "Swinging Pendulum Transfer Effect" in which one pendulum transfers its swinging energy to another pendulum, forcing it to swing. It's a wild concept. And it may help explain a lot of crazy human party behavior.

Here's how it works:

1. Make two pendulums, using Planet Dexter's exclusive rubber band and string technique explained in "The Pendulum of Fear" (page 12). Each pendulum string should be about 18 inches long.

2. Tie another string like a tightrope between two chair backs, about three feet apart.

3. Tie your two pendulums about six inches apart on the tightrope. Make sure the hanging string lengths are about equal.

4. Now, hold one pendulum still while you give the other one a push to set it swinging for a while.

5. Let go of the other pendulum but don't push it; just let it hang free.

6. Strike up the band! **Stand Back!**

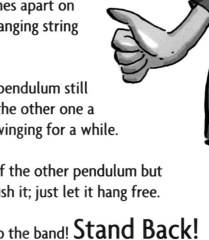

British Prime Minister John Major was actually first named John Major Ball. Somewhere along the line he dropped the Ball from his name. Which is probably why he's just a Prime Minister and not a King.

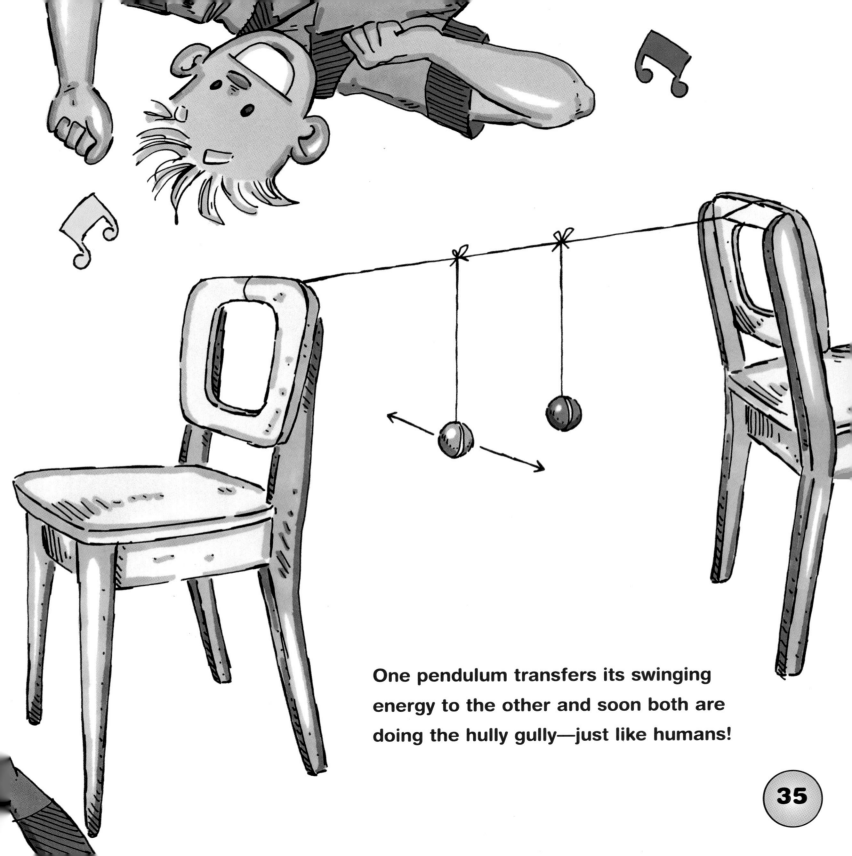

One pendulum transfers its swinging energy to the other and soon both are doing the hully gully—just like humans!

FAVORITE BALL RECIPES

Great for ball parties!

Really! Invite friends and family. Have everyone bring their favorite ball! Write out the invitation on a ball and deliver it through an open window! Play games from this book (like Gotcha Ball!—page 44). How about some ballroom dancing? Perform tricks (like the Pendulum of Fear—page 12)! Set up a volleyball net or a croquet court! Get the garden hoses out (see Getting Hosed—pages 56–59).

Have a ball!!

Matzo BALLS

INGREDIENTS

1 cup matzo meal

2 tablespoons olive oil

1 teaspoon salt

1 tablespoon chopped parsley

1 cup boiling water

1 egg, well beaten

dash of pepper

Combine matzo meal and boiling water thoroughly. Add oil, egg, salt, pepper, and parsley. Mix well and place in refrigerator for about $\frac{1}{2}$ hour. With hands wet with cold water, make balls about 1 inch in diameter. Drop into gently boiling water. Cover and cook for 25 minutes. Serve in hot soup.

Makes 16 balls.

Spaghetti and Meat**BALLS**

INGREDIENTS

1 pound ground beef

$\frac{1}{2}$ cup grated Parmesan cheese

2 small cloves garlic, minced

2 eggs, beaten

$\frac{1}{8}$ teaspoon pepper

4 tablespoons olive oil

1 cup fine dry bread crumbs

1 tablespoon minced parsley

$\frac{1}{2}$ cup milk

1 $\frac{1}{2}$ teaspoon salt

1 cup minced onion

Mix and form the above (except for the onions) into balls 1 $\frac{1}{2}$ inches in diameter. Pan-fry the balls with the onions until browned in 4 tablespoons of olive oil. Add balls to 6 cups of your favorite spaghetti sauce and simmer for about one hour. Serve over hot, drained boiled spaghetti and sprinkle heavily with grated Parmesan cheese. Makes 12 balls.

Popcorn **BALLS**

INGREDIENTS

8 cups popped corn

1 cup sugar

1/2 cup molasses

1 tablespoon butter

1/4 cup water

2 teaspoon vinegar

1/4 teaspoon salt

Put corn into a large mixing bowl. Combine the sugar, molasses, water, vinegar, and salt in a deep saucepan. Stir over low heat until sugar is almost dissolved. Cover; slowly bring to a boil. Remove cover. Boil rapidly, stirring constantly, for at least one minute, no more than two. Remove from heat and stir in butter. Pour in a fine stream over the popped corn, tossing constantly with a fork to coat all corn evenly. Grease hands lightly. Quickly shape into balls. Makes 8 to 12 balls.

GHOST KNOCKER

Sometimes you can't help it. You just want to BUG somebody. Here's something guaranteed to drive brothers, sisters, and visiting cousins BONKERS! With the Ghost Knocker, you can knock on doors WITHOUT EVEN BEING THERE!

1. Use Planet Dexter's exclusive rubber-band-and-string technique explained in "The Pendulum of Fear" (page 12). Tie about a three-foot length of string to a Superball.

2. Find a closed door with somebody behind it who desperately deserves to be bugged.

3. Tape the loose end of the string to the top of the door jamb. The ball should hang down, well within the door area.

4. Now just pull the ball toward you, let it go, and run. The ball will swing and bounce repeatedly against the door, making a knocking sound. It'll be slow at first, speeding up as the pendulum swings get quicker and quicker.

Here's what you can expect:

1. A voice inside the room murmurs "Who's there?" or "Come in."
2. The voice, louder now, repeats the request.
3. The sound of footsteps and the door opening.
4. The voice, now irate, hisses "What the . . .?!"
5. Stomping footsteps move in your direction and the sound of your name fills the air.

Note: In order to get your ball back, it may be necessary to repeat the following or similar phrase three or more times: "I promise I won't do it to you again." And promises, of course, must be kept (however, other house occupants and visitors are still fair game).

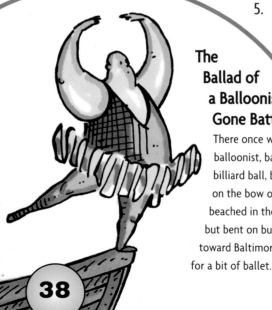

The Ballad of a Balloonist Gone Batty.

There once was a balloonist, bald as a billiard ball, balancing on the bow of a boat beached in the Baltic but bent on budging toward Baltimore for a bit of ballet.

Pendulum Power

A pendulum is a powerful thing. Just because the door in Ghost Knocker stops the pendulum's swing doesn't mean it stops the pendulum's energy. When it hits the door, the pendulum simply reverses itself and completes its swing in the opposite direction.

KICK ME!

Consider the American football.
There's nothing like it on Earth.
Well, right. But just try to kick the Goodyear Blimp through a set of goal posts.

They play various forms of football all over the world, but only in North America do we use a ball with pointed ends. Originally the ball was much more rounded—more egg-shaped—like a British rugby ball. Like rugby, American football was played mainly on the ground with very little passing. And it was brutal, with up to 25 members on each team and virtually no protective gear.

Copy Cats.

Ancient Greek athletes played a form of football called *harpaston*. Not to be outdone, the ancient Romans played a version they called *harpastum*.

It was so brutal that in 1906, a very sports-minded president, Theodore Roosevelt, told football managers to make the game safer. "Run less and pass more," the managers told their players. But it was hard to throw that big egg-shaped ball. So a smaller, pointed football was invented. The "long bomb" made football not only more thrilling, but safer.

Oh. And wearing helmets helped, too.

THERE'S MORE →

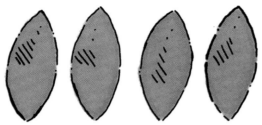

Here's a way to make an American-type football, just like the real thing. Except instead of leather, yours will be made out of paper, transparent tape and a balloon. Pass it or kick it and its pointy ends will help it easily sail through the air. That's aerodynamics.

And if it hits anything—including your head—it will do about the same amount of damage as a balloon.

1. Trace and cut four pieces of paper exactly in the shape you see on the opposite page. In a real football, these pieces would be leather.

2. Patiently tape all the seams together. Leave a space untaped in the middle of one seam, just large enough to stick an empty balloon through later.

3. By now you should have something in the general shape of a football. Stick most of the empty balloon into the football, leaving the air hole out.

4. Blow up the balloon as much as possible without breaking the seams. Tie the end of the balloon into a knot.

5. Push the knotted end of the balloon into the football and tape the open seam closed. (A real football uses a rubber bag called a bladder instead of a balloon. The open seam would be stitched shut with white cross threads.)

Fancy Word Feature

Impress Friends and Family!

aerodynamics: *noun.   The study of how gases (air) affect and interact with moving objects*

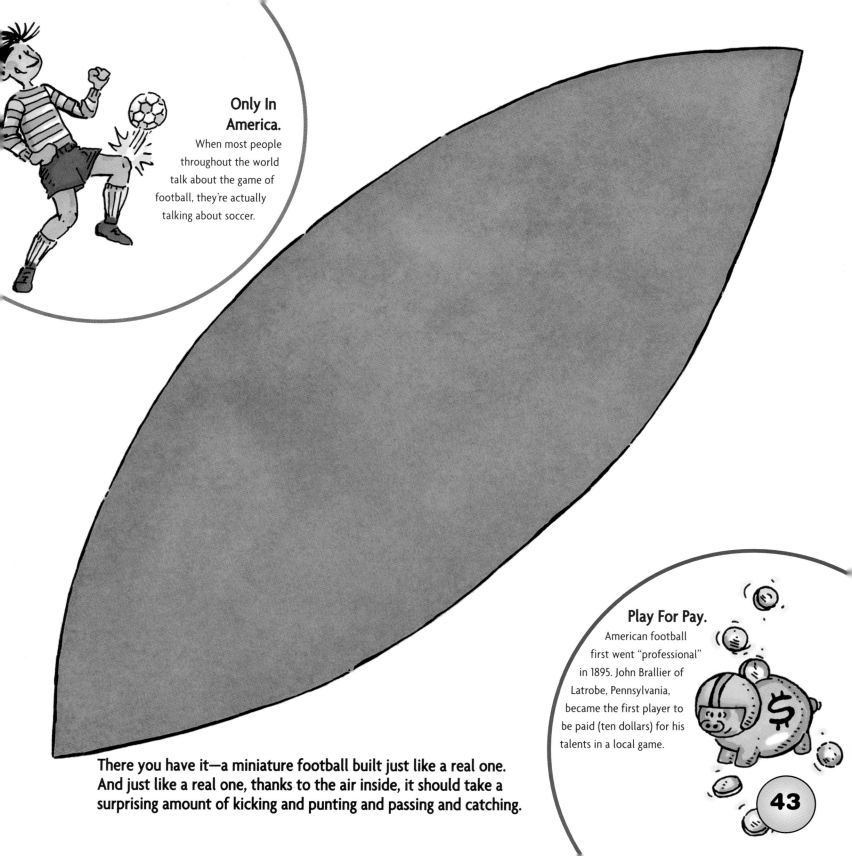

Only In America.
When most people throughout the world talk about the game of football, they're actually talking about soccer.

Play For Pay.
American football first went "professional" in 1895. John Brallier of Latrobe, Pennsylvania, became the first player to be paid (ten dollars) for his talents in a local game.

There you have it—a miniature football built just like a real one. And just like a real one, thanks to the air inside, it should take a surprising amount of kicking and punting and passing and catching.

43

GOTCHA BALL

Aircraft designers are said to be working on a jet that will travel one mile per second. That means you'll be able to fly across the Mississippi River faster than you can say "One Mississippi." One thing for sure, these planes are going to need pilots with really quick uh, you know, uh, re-, uh, reflexes and reaction times. (Hit a goose at 3000 miles per hour and you'll have a face full of goose pudding. Yuk!)

Want to fly one of those jets someday? Sure. Everybody does. Then start sharpening your reflexes right now with a game called Gotcha Ball. It works with three or more players and even 10 or so can play, making it a great party game (see appropriate party foods, page 36). You can even try it with different kinds of balls. It's great on the beach with a bowling ball. Ouch, watch your toes. We mean with a beach ball.

1. All players except one line up side by side with their arms folded.

2. The remaining player is the pitcher. He or she takes a Dexter Ball and stands about 12 feet out, facing the center of the line.

3. One by one, the pitcher selects people in line to catch the Dexter Ball. And he or she tosses it. Or just pretends to toss it, going through a tossing motion, but stopping short.

4. The target person in line has to think quickly. Target persons who don't get their arms unfolded fast enough will miss a tossed ball. They're out! Target persons who unfold their arms when the toss is fake are also out.

5. The winner is the last person left in line. He or she becomes the next pitcher.

Consistent winners of Gotcha Ball may consider themselves to have excellent reflexes.

Those wild and crazy Aztecs!

Four hundred years ago in Mexico, the Aztecs played *Ollamalitzli*, a game that closely resembled basketball. Now get a load of this: if the solid rubber ball was put through a fixed stone ring, the player who did so was entitled to the clothing of all the spectators.

45

BUMPER BALLS

Three super villains are riding together in a bumper car at a carnival. You're riding alone in your own bumper car and the villains don't see you. Suddenly, there's an opportunity to speed up and smash into the villains' car while they're standing still. Smashing into three super villains at once! You'll be a hero!

Just as you're ready to strike, the alarm clock rings. Luck of a squid! It was a dream! All day long you're stuck guessing what that triumphant collision would have been like.

Well, forget it. You're lucky you woke up. The problem? Well, let's demonstrate.

1. Put a Superball and a Ping-Pong ball three or four inches apart on a table. The heavier Superball represents the mass of the three large villains squeezed into the bumper car. The lighter Ping-Pong ball is you, riding alone.

2. Flick the villains' car into yours. (Flick the Superball into the Ping-Pong ball.) Observe . . . a collision that villains might dream about, no?

3. Now, flick your car into the villain's car. (Flick the Ping-Pong ball into the Superball.) What happens?

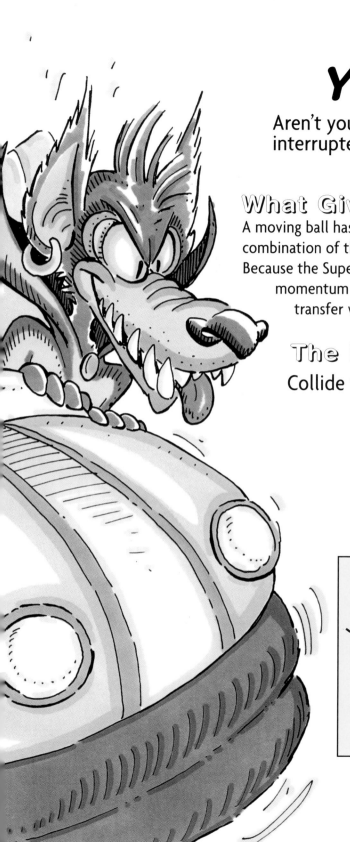

Yikes!

Aren't you glad the alarm clock interrupted your dream?

What Gives?

A moving ball has momentum, which is a combination of the ball's mass and speed. Because the Superball has more mass, it has more momentum when it's moving, and more momentum to transfer when it hits the Ping-Pong ball.

The Moral of the Story:

Collide with super villains one at a time.

Impress Friends and Family!

mass: *noun.*   1) *The measure of a body's resistance to acceleration; the mass of a body is different from but proportional to its weight (for example, a pound of feathers weighs the same as a pound of cement, but masses sure are different!) and may be expressed in mass units, as kilograms or slugs (slugs?! gross!);*
2) *One of those religious services (If you don't like this definition, try the one on page 6!).*

STEP RIGHT UP!
YOU TOO CAN WIN VALUABLE PRIZES!

Wouldn't it be great to win one of those huge, stuffed bears or dinosaurs or Bart Simpsons they have at carnivals? You know, the ones that are three feet wide and six feet tall and take up all the space in your room? Wow! What could be better? Well, stop dreaming and start winning!

Here's how!

The Milk Bottle Game

You usually have to throw a softball and completely knock down a pyramid of three aluminum bottles. It looks simple, but sometimes one or both bottles on the bottom are weighted so they don't go down easily. Carnival experts say your best bet is to aim directly for the area where the three bottles meet.

The Basketball Game

Michael Jordan couldn't win a key chain on some of these basketball rigs. That's because some carnival operators have been known to tilt or loosen the rim a bit so balls bounce off in wacky directions instead of banking into the hoop. Forget about bank shots—go for a swish every time. And keep an eye out for over-inflated balls and under-sized rims, too.

Speaking of Villains . . .

Ever see a lottery drawing on television? Numbered Ping-Pong balls bounce around in an air machine until some pop up out of the mix to show the winning numbers. Well, once upon a time the host of the Pennsylvania Lottery decided to help his buddies win. He took a syringe and injected white paint into some of the Ping-Pong balls, making them heavier. He then told his friends to bet on the lighter balls. His scheme worked until the number of his "friends" grew a little too large. Our "host" made a lot of new friends in jail.

Take that, Michael Jordan.

On February 5, 1974, Mats Wermelin, age 13, scored all 272 points in a 272–0 win at a regional basketball tournament in Stockholm, Sweden.

49

FIGHTING GRAVITY WITH MAYONNAISE

trickery!   food!   victory!

The first step in **"Fighting Gravity with Mayonnaise"** is to invite all your friends over for sandwiches. Turkey, roast beef, cheese, and ham are best served smothered in the white, oily concoction. Keep eating. After enough sandwiches, you'll have an empty mayonnaise jar and a bloated crowd ready for entertainment. **No problem!**

Just wash out the mayonnaise jar and dry it inside and out. Place it upside down on a tabletop over one of your Super Balls. Begin swirling the jar around the ball, keeping the mouth of the jar in contact with the tabletop. Eventually, the ball will rise up into the mayonnaise jar and roll around the inside of the jar. When this happens, continue swirling and you can actually lift the bottle off the table with the ball spinning smoothly around the inside of the jar.

Wow! — sandwiches and a demonstration of fearless gravity-fighting: it's a crowd-pleasing combo.

Is It Really a Victory Over Gravity?

Absolutely! Gravity wants to keep the ball on the table, and you're using centrifugal force against gravitational force. When an object spins, centrifugal force wants to pull it outward. In fact, it's a fine balance of gravity and centrifugal force that keeps satellites in orbit.

The I-Hate-Mayonnaise! Issue

You can try other jars large enough to accommodate a ball rolling around inside. Any jar with a mouth a little narrower than the sides of the jar will work. Try a pickle jar (great for sandwich parties).

DEXTABLE TENNIS

The noble game of Ping-Pong or table tennis was first played about 100 years ago on dining-room tables with improvised equipment. That's funny, because on Planet Dexter it's still played like that.

Everybody's dining-room or kitchen table is different, but here are some basic ideas to let you improvise a game of table tennis any time you want. Just make sure you have enough room to swing your paper-plate paddles.

All you need:

- Two paper plates for each player
- One table; two chairs
- Stapler, string, newspaper, and scissors
- Your Ping-Pong ball

Get Paddled

Staple two paper plates together to make a paddle. Cut a slot at one edge just big enough to stick your hand in.

Net Work

Place the two chairs across from each other at the table's midpoint. Stretch and tie a string between the two chairs, six inches above the table. Cut a newspaper sheet lengthwise along its crease and place it over the string to make a net.

The Complicated Rules

Just hit the ball back and forth over the net, bouncing it once on the opponent's side before the opponent hits it back. When hitting the ball for the first time (called "the serve"), the ball should bounce once on the server's side. Play continues until a player:

- misses the ball,
- hits the ball into the net,
- hits the ball off the table without bouncing it on the opponent's side, or
- badmouths Planet Dexter.

If any of these four things happens, the other player gets a point. After every 5 points, the other person becomes the server. The first person to reach 21 points wins.

The Easy Rules

Just see how long you and your friend can keep the ball going.
This is called "volleying."

Can You Imagine Doing ANYTHING
5000 times?

5000 is said to be the record number of
consecutive volleys anyone's ever achieved in
table tennis.

SKY BALL

A lively conversation is overheard in the food court at Riverside Mountain Valley Oceanfront Mall:

Kid A: "I can make winter boots out of butter tubs!"

Kid B: "I can make a hat out of an egg carton!"

Kid C: "I can make a Ping-Pong ball levitate over my head!"

If you identify with Kid A or Kid B, then you're in the wrong book. This is where we levitate Ping-Pong balls over our heads. Really. And if you've never had a crick in your neck before, get ready, because you're going to get one now. This little maneuver will have you looking up at the sky or ceiling for hours. In fact, don't even try this if it's anywhere near meal time. You won't be able to stop . . . and why go hungry?

Just blow long and hard through a drinking straw pointed straight up. While you're blowing, place a Ping- Pong ball right in the stream of air. Think the ball will go flying off across the room? Or might it do something just a bit unearthly?

Hmmmmm?
How high can you get it?
How long can you keep it going?

Don't forget to inhale.

Hey, kids!—what's going on here?

It's all a matter of Bernoulli's principle, which states that the faster the flow of air, the lower the pressure. The air under the ball— the air coming from the straw—has less strength than all the other air around the ball. This keeps the ball in place, preventing it from shooting right up through the ceiling, out the roof, and into Mr. Wilson's backyard.

Could a tennis ball stay afloat all the way from Pittsburgh, where the Ohio River starts, down past Cincinnati, through St. Louis where the Ohio flows into the Mississippi, and all the way to New Orleans where that big old river dumps into the Gulf of Mexico? What do you think? If you live in Pittsburgh and have a good friend in New Orleans, maybe the two of you could check this out and report back. See page 7 for how to contact us. And hey, thanks!

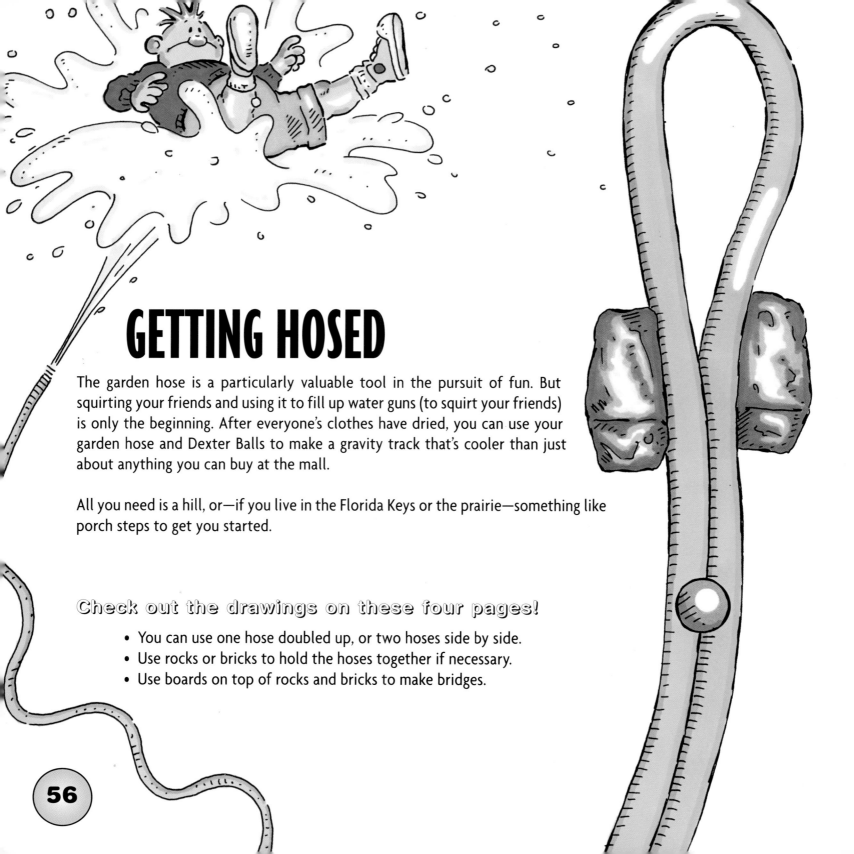

GETTING HOSED

The garden hose is a particularly valuable tool in the pursuit of fun. But squirting your friends and using it to fill up water guns (to squirt your friends) is only the beginning. After everyone's clothes have dried, you can use your garden hose and Dexter Balls to make a gravity track that's cooler than just about anything you can buy at the mall.

All you need is a hill, or—if you live in the Florida Keys or the prairie—something like porch steps to get you started.

Check out the drawings on these four pages!

- You can use one hose doubled up, or two hoses side by side.
- Use rocks or bricks to hold the hoses together if necessary.
- Use boards on top of rocks and bricks to make bridges.

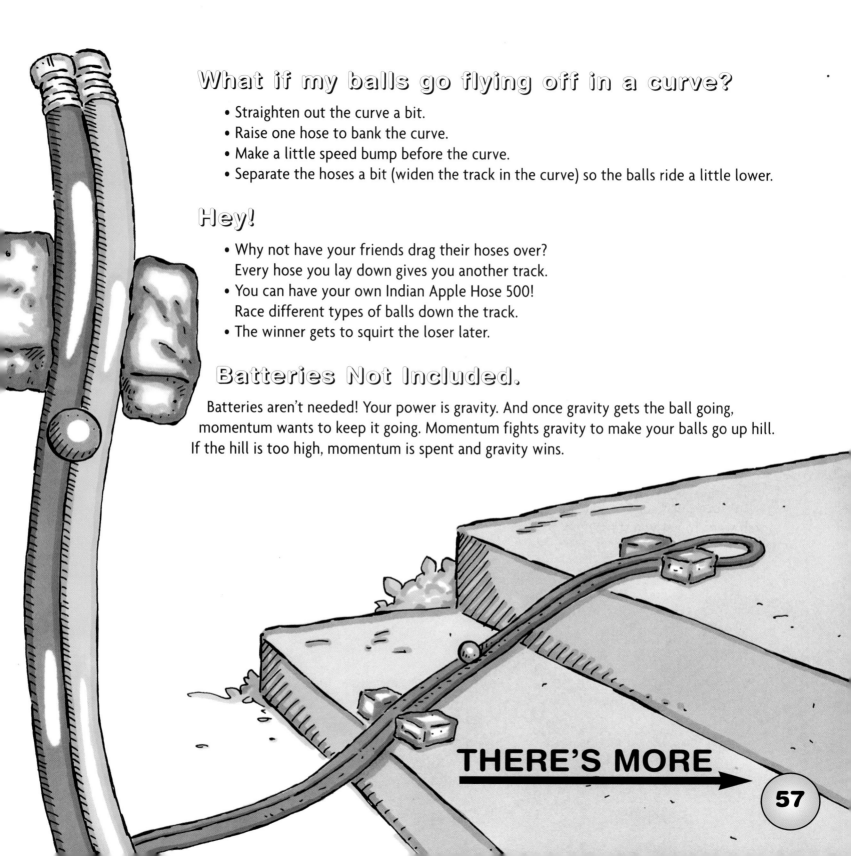

What if my balls go flying off in a curve?

- Straighten out the curve a bit.
- Raise one hose to bank the curve.
- Make a little speed bump before the curve.
- Separate the hoses a bit (widen the track in the curve) so the balls ride a little lower.

Hey!

- Why not have your friends drag their hoses over?
  Every hose you lay down gives you another track.
- You can have your own Indian Apple Hose 500!
  Race different types of balls down the track.
- The winner gets to squirt the loser later.

Batteries Not Included.

Batteries aren't needed! Your power is gravity. And once gravity gets the ball going, momentum wants to keep it going. Momentum fights gravity to make your balls go up hill. If the hill is too high, momentum is spent and gravity wins.

THERE'S MORE →

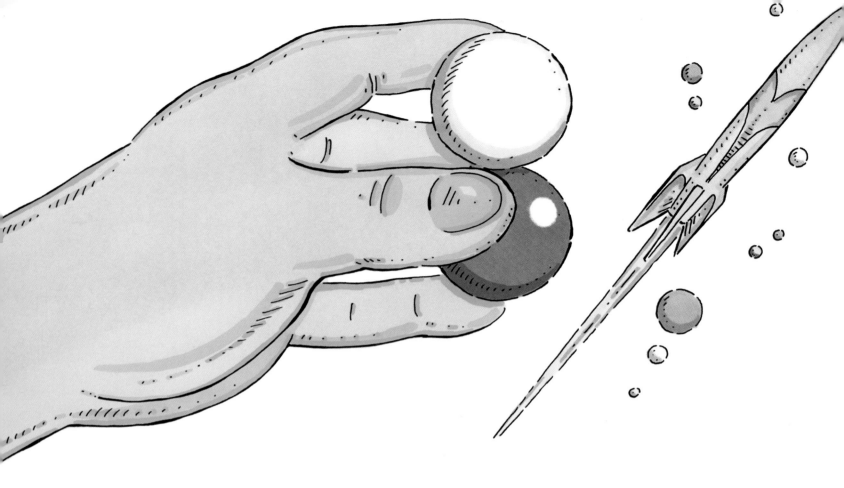

ACHIEVING ORBIT

By now you're pretty familiar with the bouncing abilities
of your Superball and Ping-Pong ball.

**(Superball—"dooomp, dooomp;"
Ping-Pong ball—"click, kaclick.")**

Well, it's supercharging time!

Hold your Ping-Pong ball on top of your Superball. Drop them onto a hard surface so the two stay together on the way down.

pA-DOOOIIIINNNNGGG!

What has gotten into that Ping-Pong ball?

Hey, kids!—what's going on here?

It has to do with **momentum** (check back to "Why can't you throw a Ping-Pong ball as far as a baseball if you can throw a baseball much further than a shot put?" on page 10). As the two balls drop, the Superball picks up more momentum (because it has more mass) than the Ping-Pong ball. When the Superball hits the floor, all of its many particles are squeezed like tiny springs. When all those squeezed particles prepare to bounce back to their original shapes, that momentum is transferred over to the Ping-Pong ball, sending it flying off like crazy. It's as if you're dancing nice and tight with somebody and suddenly your partner gets bumped into, and you go flying off like a Ping-Pong ball and land in the punch bowl. Well, maybe.

A kooky Australian experiment in which a giant Superball was dropped off a skyscraper was a real bomb. The huge ball cracked on impact, sending jagged pieces bounding down the street and through shop and office windows.

ALL THINGS BALL-SY

Between . . .

. . . 1950 and 1978, Francis A. Johnson built a string ball 12 feet, 9 inches in diameter, 40 feet in circumference, and weighing 11 tons.

. . . August 12th and 25th, Peter del Maste dribbled a basketball 265.2 miles from Lee, Massachusetts, to Provincetown, Massachusetts.

If you do a lot of traveling

(or live in a really diversified neighborhood) . . .

How to say "Ball" in 16 different languages (lang-gwij-is)

Czech:	miç (mitts)
Danish:	bold (boolt)
Dutch:	bol (bowl)
Finnish:	pallo (pah-lo)
Greek:	bvl (vol)
Hawaiian:	kinipopo (key-knee-poh-poh)
Hungarian:	golyÓ (gohl-yo)
Italian:	palla (paal-a)
Polish:	pilka (peel-ka)
Portuguese:	bala (bahl-a)
Romanian:	bila (beal-a)
Serbo-Croatian:	lopta (loh-ohp-ta)
Spanish:	bola (bowl-ah)
Swedish:	boll (bowl)
Turkish:	top (toap)
Welsh:	pel (peh-l)

Balls and the Media . . .

"It's hard to generalize about what makes balls fun, but at least sometimes it must be the sheer mastery of solving, with eyes and hands, whatever impossible calculus problem sums up the trajectory of a thrown or bounced projectile."
— James Gleick, *The New York Times*, (a newspaper with no comics section)

In . . .

. . . 1984, some guy named Albert Lucas juggled ten balls simultaneously.

. . . 1962, Australian meteorologist Nils Lied hit the longest golf drive ever: 2,640 yards, about 1 1/2 miles (across ice in Antarctica).

. . . 1987, Tony Ferko of Czechoslovakia juggled seven Ping-Pong balls with his mouth.